20 Questions

A Self-Reflection Journal for Jesus-Followers
That Will Make You Think

By Rich Speeney & Tyler Heath

ISBN: 9781731286444

Start here.

I don't like devotional books.

Over the years I've spent following Jesus, I've read plenty of them, and most fall into one of two categories:

1. Flowery, inspirational pep talk
2. Basic, Sunday school instructions

While their content can be uplifting and theologically accurate, they're not helpful for following Jesus in real life.

I appreciate the encouragement of devos from the first category, but I struggle to reconcile their comforting self-help talk with the words of Jesus.

Like when He says, "If anyone comes to me and does not hate his own father and mother and wife and children and brothers and sisters, yes, and even his own life, he cannot be my disciple."[1] Ouch.

The other type is great in theory or if you're eight years old, but when faith collides with the real world, Sunday school answers fall short.

Christianity is about far more than having an upbeat attitude and accepting a mindless faith that points you only to moral improvement.

Tyler and I have created something different. We're not gonna tell you what to do. No preaching. No hitting you over the head with The Bible.

Our goal is **to provoke humble reflection that prompts you to love like Jesus.**

We want to guide you to deeper and richer experience as a follower of Jesus because as you become more like Christ, you'll increasingly experience what it means to be human. As you live the life of love that God intends and Jesus models, you'll experience an incomparable joy, peace, and satisfaction.

20 Questions is designed for people of all ages and stages of their journey with Jesus. If you're interested in exploring how following Jesus impacts your daily life, this journal is for you. It's intended to be used over a twenty-day period. Each day includes a question, a few sentences that express the heart behind the question, a quote from a hero of our faith, and space for you to reflect.

Each question helps you think about your faith in your *current stage of life*, so you can revisit these questions over time to continue to push you closer to Christ.

Why a journal? Because meaningful growth happens when you think for **yourself.**

Jesus wasn't known for His monologues as much as He was for His questions. Over and over, He handled situations not with 45-minute sermons, but with meaningful questions that provoked self-reflection and activated change. His questions, always rooted in truth, were catalysts for deeper faith and self-discovery in His listeners.

Over the next twenty days, we're going to help you think for yourself. No lectures, just raw, honest reflection.

At points it'll be comforting, and at points it'll be convicting. We've stripped away the hazy Christian lingo that permeates the Christian subculture and replaced it with normal, everyday language to help you gain new perspectives on topics you've processed before.

Not convinced about journaling? We're not the only ones to believe in its power. Credible researchers agree that journaling benefits the mind, body, and soul. It helps you know yourself better by clarifying your thoughts and feelings; it reduces stress and anxiety and helps you recognize and prioritize the opportunities and challenges in your life.[2]

Our questions emphasize actions, but Christianity isn't about what you do.

It's about *who you are.*

Regardless of what you've done and what you'll do, good or bad, **you are loved by God.**

Here's the good news: Jesus already did everything that needs to be done! So breathe, relax, and rest in that freedom.

Why do we focus on actions? Because your actions are an expression of your heart. And as your heart begins to change and reflect the heart of Jesus, you'll experience a **"rich and satisfying life."[3]**

Trust the process and enjoy the journey.

- Rich

1

What are you thankful for?

On even the worst days, you can be thankful for something. Reflect on the people, resources, and opportunities you take for granted and the ways you can express your gratitude to God and others.

_____

_____

_____

_____

_____

_____

_____

_____

_____

_____

_____

_____

_____

_____

_____

_____

_____
_____
_____
_____
_____
_____
_____
_____
_____
_____
_____
_____
_____
_____
_____
_____
_____
_____
_____
_____
_____
_____
_____
_____
_____

"Give thanks in all circumstances; for this is God's will for you in Christ Jesus." - Paul

2 How would Jesus live and engage in your culture?

Jesus didn't isolate himself from the world. He participated in the everyday rhythms of the places He went, yet He didn't let the world around Him change His character or mission. Reflect on how Jesus would live in your school, work place, city, and neighborhood and how you can live like Him.

_____

_____

_____

_____

_____

_____

_____

_____

_____

_____

_____

_____

_____

_____

_____

_____

_____

_____

_____

_____

_____

_____

_____

_____

_____

_____

_____

_____

_____

_____

_____

_____

_____

_____

_____

_____

_____

_____

"Don't copy the behavior and customs of this world, but let God transform you into a new person by changing the way you think." - Paul

3

What do you pray for?

Conversations reveal a lot about relationships. Reflect on what the content of your conversations with God says about you and the way you relate to Him.

_____

_____

_____

_____

_____

_____

_____

_____

_____

_____

_____

_____

_____

_____

_____

_____

_____

"Ask and it will be given to you; seek and you will find; knock and the door will be opened to you." - Jesus

4

What do you do when no one is looking?

What you do in secret says a lot about your character. Reflect on how you act when there aren't visible rewards or consequences.

_____

_____

_____

_____

_____

_____

_____

_____

_____

_____

_____

_____

_____

_____

_____

_____

_____

_____

"Your Father, who sees what is done in secret, will reward you."
- Jesus

5

What does your calendar say about how you resemble Jesus?

How you spend your time says a lot about your priorities. Reflect on your schedule and how it reflects the desires of your heart.

_____

_____

_____

_____

_____

_____

_____

_____

_____

_____

_____

_____

_____

_____

_____

_____

_____

"Look carefully then how you walk, not as unwise but as wise, making the best use of the time." - Paul

6

How are you actively using your skills and talents for the benefit of others?

God made you good at something. Reflect on how you're helping others with your abilities and expertise.

_____

_____

_____

_____

_____

_____

_____

_____

_____

_____

_____

_____

_____

_____

_____

_____

"Each of you should use whatever gift you have received to serve others." - Peter

7

What masks are you hiding behind?

Jesus set you free from pretending to be something you're not. Reflect on your insecurities, how you attempt to cover them up, and how you can move forward in freedom.

_____

_____

_____

_____

_____

_____

_____

_____

_____

_____

_____

_____

_____

_____

_____

_____

"Christ has truly set us free." - Paul

8

Who is training you?
Who are you training?

A disciple is a lifelong learner and a lifelong teacher. Reflect on who you are intentionally investing into and who is intentionally investing in you.

_____

_____

_____

_____

_____

_____

_____

_____

_____

_____

_____

_____

_____

_____

_____

_____

_____

"Go and make disciples of all the nations...teach these new disciples to obey all the commands I have given you." - Jesus

9

What is God jealous for in your life?

If Christ is not at the center of your heart, something else is. Reflect on the things you're tempted to love more than God.

_____

_____

_____

_____

_____

_____

_____

_____

_____

_____

_____

_____

_____

_____

_____

_____

_____

"For people will be...lovers of pleasure rather than lovers of God, having the appearance of godliness, but denying its power."
- Paul

10 Would you and Jesus have mutual friends?

Jesus liked people that were nothing like Him. And they liked Him back. He spent His weekends with social outcasts and people that were rough around the edges. Reflect on how you imitate Jesus as a friend of all people.

_____

_____

_____

_____

_____

_____

_____

_____

_____

_____

_____

_____

_____

_____

_____

_____

"The Son of Man came eating and drinking, and you [Pharisees] say, 'Here is a glutton and a drunkard, a friend of tax collectors and sinners.'" - Jesus

11 How is the enemy working against you?

The mission of God directly opposes the mission of the enemy, so if you're pursuing God's mission, the enemy will be working against you. Reflect on the ways the enemy is attempting to distract and derail you from living a life of love.

_____

_____

_____

_____

_____

_____

_____

_____

_____

_____

_____

_____

_____

_____

_____

_____

_____

"Your enemy the devil prowls around like a roaring lion looking for someone to devour." - Peter

12

What would it look like for you to be more dependent on God?

Most of us cogitatively recognize our need for God, yet we don't want to count on anyone but ourselves. Reflect on what action you can take to deeper rely on God, letting Him meet all your needs.

_____

_____

_____

_____

_____

_____

_____

_____

_____

_____

_____

_____

_____

_____

_____

_____

_____

"If you remain in me and I in you, you will bear much fruit; apart from me you can do nothing." - Jesus

13 What are you sacrificing to follow Jesus?

Jesus was clear: reorienting your life around Him will be costly. Reflect on what you're currently giving up because of your faith in Christ.

_____

_____

_____

_____

_____

_____

_____

_____

_____

_____

_____

_____

_____

_____

_____

_____

_____

_____

_____

_____

_____

_____

_____

_____

_____

_____

_____

_____

_____

_____

_____

_____

_____

_____

_____

_____

_____

_____

"Whoever wants to be my disciple must deny themselves and take up their cross and follow me." - Jesus

14

Who do you need to forgive? What bitterness and resentment are you holding on to?

God's love keeps no record of wrongs. Reflect on the hurt you're hanging on to and how you can forgive as Christ forgave you.

_____

_____

_____

_____

_____

_____

_____

_____

_____

_____

_____

_____

_____

_____

_____

"Be kind and compassionate to one another, forgiving each other, just as in Christ God forgave you." - Paul

15

What does your bank statement say about how you resemble Jesus?

The way you spend your money says a lot about your priorities. Reflect on how Jesus would reallocate your income and expenses.

_____

_____

_____

_____

_____

_____

_____

_____

_____

_____

_____

_____

_____

_____

_____

_____

_____

_____

_____

_____

_____

_____

_____

_____

_____

_____

_____

_____

_____

_____

_____

_____

_____

_____

_____

_____

_____

"For where your treasure is, there your heart will be also." - Jesus

16

What do your actions indicate about your definition of success?

If a stranger observed every moment of your life, what would he/she think you were trying to achieve? Reverse engineer your definition of success by reflecting on your daily actions and what these actions reveal about what you're chasing.

_____

_____

_____

_____

_____

_____

_____

_____

_____

_____

_____

_____

_____

_____

_____

_____

_____

_____

"Let's not merely say that we love each other; let us show the truth by our actions." - John

17 What worries you?

When you trust that God is loving and in control, you'll find you have no reason to worry. Reflect on the daily fears and anxieties that consume your thoughts and emotions and how you can release control to God.

"There is no fear in love, but perfect love casts out fear. For fear has to do with punishment, and whoever fears has not been perfected in love." - John

18

What would your life look like if you weren't a Jesus-follower?

Compare your current life as a Christian to what your current life would look like if you weren't a Christian and reflect on the difference.

_____

_____

_____

_____

_____

_____

_____

_____

_____

_____

_____

_____

_____

_____

_____

_____

_____

_____

"Anyone who belongs to Christ has become a new person. The old life is gone; a new life has begun!" - Paul

19 Who do you neglect to love?

Jesus' love was unconditional and expressed in tangible ways. Reflect on what individuals and people groups would say about your love for them.

_____

_____

_____

_____

_____

_____

_____

_____

_____

_____

_____

_____

_____

_____

_____

_____

_____

_____

"I am giving you a new commandment: Love each other." - Jesus

20

What do others experience when they encounter you?

Our behavior towards others is an expression of our character. Reflect on what vibe you give off and how you make people feel in your daily interactions.

_____

_____

_____

_____

_____

_____

_____

_____

_____

_____

_____

_____

_____

_____

_____

_____

_____

"Just as I have loved you, you should love each other." - Jesus

Notes

Introduction:
1 – Luke 14:26
2 – University of Rochester Medical Center (https://www.ur-mc.rochester.edu/encyclopedia/content.aspx?ContentID=4552&ContentTypeID=1)
3 – John 10:10

Questions:
1 – 1 Thessalonians 5:18
2 – Romans 12:2
3 – Luke 11:9
4 – Matthew 16:18
5 – Ephesians 5:15-16
6 – 1 Peter 4:10
7 – Galatians 5:1
8 – Matthew 28:19-20
9 – 1 Timothy 3:2-5
10 – Luke 7:34
11 – 1 Peter 5:8
12 – John 15:5
13 – Matthew 16:24
14 – Ephesians 4:32
15 – Matthew 6:21
16 – 1 John 3:18
17 – 1 John 4:18
18 – 2 Corinthians 5:17
19 – John 13:34
20 – John 13:34

Made in the USA
Monee, IL
12 December 2019